RIVERSONG

by

LEE UNDERWOOD

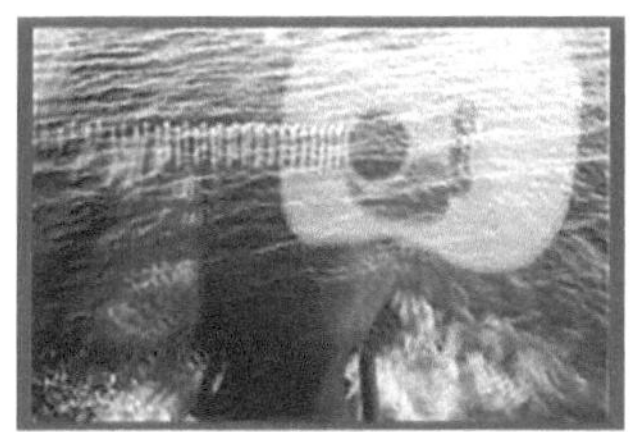

Poetic Matrix Press
www.poeticmatrix.com

Credits

Cover picture — Troy Desbians
Sonia photo — Lee Underwood
Solo guitar photo — Lee Underwood
Playing guitar, white hat, yellow shirt — Rusty Crutcher

RIVERSONG

INTRODUCTION

Nearly all of the poems included in Riversong are new. They are expressions of personal love, transcendental realization, and my deep involvement with nature and music.

STREAM…RIVER…FLOW, that starts off the FOREVER SONGS Section, for example, is a journey from youth's first realization of the power of music, when as a nine-year-old boy, lying in bed, I held a plastic radio up to my ear, listening to "The Grand Ol' Opry," and heard for the first time the magical guitar of Chet Atkins. I had never heard anything remotely like what he was doing with his music. I was transported into the first heaven I had ever known.

That musical experience awakened me to the realization that life itself is a stream, a river, an eternal flowng that forever surrounds us and infuses us and carries us through waves of music, which only sometimes do we become aware of. Life is a RIVERSONG filled with light, fire, and beauty. Life itself is that RIVERSONG.

As my life streamed on, other adventures appeared to me in that music flow — such as running away from home in Big Spring west Texas as a 14-year-old boy, hitch-hiking to Memphis, stealing a row boat, and sailing down the Mississippi River.

That journey was the first of many adventures that river-streamed through my life, including learning how to drink beer as a college student, how to make love, and, later on, how to play guitar, which hearkened me back to the music of Chet Atkins. STREAM…RIVER…FLOW also includes a mini-biography of my journey as the lead guitarist with a "wild-haired singer" (which some readers will recognize as Tim Buckley.)

Memory plays a role in many of these poems — memories of physical and emotional love, of watching the mind-stream's magical twists and turns, of sorrow, of hope, and of ultimate transcendence, as in WAITING… WATCHING… LISTENING. Or, as in NEW MOONS — we face memories

*that leave us locked in dreams that keep us from growing —
except when we step out of those fantasies, and caste our
eyes up at the night-sky and sense the incredible beauty, the
magnificence of "these glistening planets and those sailing
comets." Our busy mind suddenly stops — and we hear the
wind that blows across the span of our mind and our life —
this, too, is the music of the RIVERSONG.*

*LADY OF THE STREAMS, the poem that opens the
LADY OF THE STREAMS Section offers a brief biography of
my late wife, Sonia Crespi, who was born in Brooklyn, but
who discovered her true self while camping in the Colo-
rado mountains. She moved from her self-with-memories
into her deepest authentic self while sitting alone beside
a stream while I was out fishing. This was a monumental
change — from the inner busyness of her mind, to a silent,
fully awakened inner life. She glowed with light, especially
when she smiled. It was as if she had been born anew. She
was radiant.*

*LADY OF THE STREAMS Section also recalls her life
and the love we shared over 50 years, leading up to her
death on December 26, 2022, the day after Christmas, a
little more than a month before her 88th birthday. INTO
BOUNDLESS SILENCE describes her death and my response
to it, leading the reader through my shock and eventual
recovery. WALKING WITH NEW EYES and THE CLOSING
CHAPTER finally helped me remember that "Everything lies
ahead/There is no past, only an ascending now."*

*The HEAT, HEART, AND FIRE Section — starts with
HEAT, HEART, AND FIRE, which leads in turn to ELECTRIC
WORDS, NIGHT RYDER DREAM-SONGS and several other
poems dealing with some of my efforts to reach out to others.*

*In the RIVERSONG Section, the title poem RIVER-
SONG, which bemoans the fact that the music I heard on
the TV or on the radio brought only memories that inev-
itably took me backwards in time. But when "I sink back
into the river's flow/The time is here-now forever." In THE
THOUSAND-YEARS WOES, I note that every year closer to*

the grave is also a year closer to the ultimate fulfillment of "every note I have played, every word I have written/And all of the love I have given — and received." In "A FLAME-SPEAR'S LIGHT I ultimately find quietude "in the music of my soul."

Some may find they have read a few of these poems in one of my three poetry books (Timewinds, 2010; Diamondfire, 2016; Into Light, 2021). Facebook friends may also recognize some of the poems I have posted along the way. But as I said above, nearly all of the poems included in RIVERSONGS are of a recent vintage.

I do hope you enjoy the journey. There is something about the written word that can be magical, uplifting, even transformational. I trust you will find something of the same in these poems. Very best to you and yours — and keep on keepin' on!

DEDICATION

SONIA CRESPI

February 5, 1935 — December 26, 2022

To my beloved wife of 50 years,
I dedicate Riversong and all of my
other published and unpublished works.
She was the one who made them come alive.
I feel most blessed to have loved her,
even as she loved me deeply and truly.

MUSIC

*Music arises in the cosmos and sings throughout
the universe. On our small blue globe, each note
blossoms into a culture, each flower into a musician,
each leaf into a song.*

*Just like a poem, a child, an orchid, a dove, a planet, a star,
a galaxy — music in all of its manifestations exists above our
human commotion and sings with a life of its own.*

*Music, a vital power, the breath of being, is as beautiful and
indestructible as cosmic joy itself. With all of our ups and
downs, life IS our personal riversong.*

Listeners who seek its music will find it within themselves.

Those who listen well will always hear it.

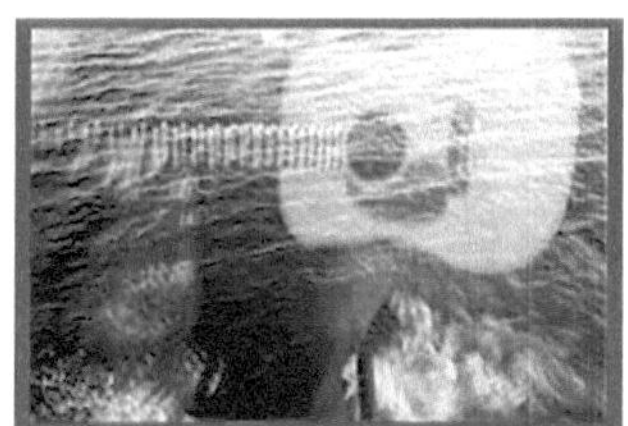

RIVERSONG

INTRODUCTION
DEDICATION
MUSIC

FOREVER SONGS

STREAM. . .RIVER. . .FLOW. . .   ~1~
TOGETHER: ONE   ~5~
RIVER TIME FLOWS TOWARD THE FALLS   ~6~
SING   ~7~
FOREVER-SONGS   ~8~
FLIGHT OF GEESE   ~9~
MOVING THROUGH THE SCRAPBOOKS   ~10~
NEW MOONS   ~11~
WAITING. . .WATCHING. . .LISTENING   ~12~
SINGING FOR THE NOW   ~14~
DIAMONDFIRE HEARTSONG   ~15~

LADY OF THE STREAMS

LADY OF THE STREAMS   ~19~
THE WAYS OF TIME AND JOY   ~24~
TOGETHER ALWAYS   ~26~
LIGHT BEYOND THE SUN   ~28~
NO OTHER LOVE   ~29~
ONLY YOU KNEW   ~30~
WE ARE ONE   ~32~
DRINK, SMOKE, SLEEP   ~33~
INTO BOUNDLESS SILENCE   ~34~
THIS TEAR-DROP MOMENT   ~37~
FOREVER   ~38~
LOVE AND GRIEF   ~39~
GOODNIGHT KISSES   ~40~
NEW YELLOW FLOWERS   ~41~
LEAVE A CANDLE BURNING   ~42~

LISTEN WITHOUT THOUGHT ~43~
RIVERRUSH TO STILLPOINT ~45~

HEAT, HEART, AND FIRE

HEAT, HEART, AND FIRE ~51~
ELECTRIC WORDS ~52~
NITE RYDER DREAM-SONGS ~53~
SUNLIGHT'S INVALUABLE PROMISE ~54~
WORD-TOUCH ELECTRONIC FIRE ~56~
BEAUTIFULLY AND TRULY FOREVER ~57~
SWEET ANGELS ~59~
SEEK ME AND FIND YOURSELF ~61~
A RINGING MOUNTAIN GONG ~63~
I WILL NEVER FADE AWAY ~65~
WALKING, WITH NEW EYES ~67~
THE CLOSING CHAPTER ~69~

RIVERSONGS

WATCHING ~75~
A FLAME-SPEAR'S LIGHT ~76~
RIVERSONG ~77~
WITHIN THIS SHINING NOW ~79~
ALL THINGS FLOW ~80~
THE THOUSAND-YEARS WOES ~81~
STAND WITHIN THE STARS ~83~
TAO ~86~
THE CANOE RIDER ~87~

ABOUT THE POET

FOREVER SONGS

STREAM. . .RIVER. . .FLOW. . .

The music began when I was lying in bed,
A nine-year-old boy listening to
The Grand Ol' Opry through a
Tiny plastic radio held close to my ear
At night when I was supposed to be asleep—
When Chet Atkins came on playing his guitar —
It was music from another world.
I had never heard such clear melodies,
And such luminous chords —
His rainbow guitar-song swept me up and away—
  His music changed my life.

Streaming. . .

At the age of 14, a friend of mine and I
Ran away from home (leaving a note for my parents).
We hitch-hiked through West Texas,
To Memphis, where in the dark midnight hour,
We ran through a nightman's search-light
Into the shadows where the boats were kept.
We untied a row boat from a cruiser, hopped in,
Began our journey down the Mississippi River —
But bargemen passing by us had alerted cops
Who greeted us in Helena, Arkansas,
And threw us in jail, called my folks,
Who drove out and took us home —
  Humiliated on the one hand,
  But victorious on the other. . .

Streaming. . .Streaming. . .Streaming. . .

CONTINUE

I discovered the delights of alcohol
In my second year of college.
I had a beer. . . Umm. . .Had a second beer.
Then took a full jug of beer back into
A dark corner in a back room, and there,
In the shadows, alone, drank the whole thing,
Delighting in the sensual way it felt
Going from my mouth, down into my throat,
A sensual connection to streams
Like I had known only fishing in
Colorado mountains — between the fish
And myself — the connection: at one.

Streaming. . .Streaming. . . Rivering. . .

My longing for freedom,
My yearning for transcendence
After lying in bed listening to
Chet Atkin's spinning
Majestic musical luminations
Through the little plastic radio
Into my awakening ear. . .
Release — freedom, yes—
That's what that music gave me:
I was bedazzled by the feeling
Of being released into freedom!

And after being emboldened by
my journey down the Mississippi —
I was now ready for more exhilaration,
        Ready for more beer—
        Ready to look across the table,

CONTINUE

~2~

Stare into the young eyes of an awakening girl,
Ready for music to swirl me, the ache of sex,
The expression of look, see, touch, feel,
And yes ready for the sweet release —
Ready for a new freedom!

Rivering. . .Riverflow. . . River-flowing. . .

Later, in New York,
A wild-haired singer-songwriter
Dropped into my life, heard me play guitar,
Asked me to join his band. I listened to him,
Dazzled by his singing, dazzled by his mind,
Dazzled by the heart he gave —
From that life-changing moment on,
I gave everything I could of myself —

The books I had read, the music I had heard,
The intelligence that infused him and me —
And lo and behold, that journey was the answer
To my midnight dream-wanderings as a boy
With his little plastic radio hugged close to his ear,
A boy whose imagination and yearning for transcendence,
Were aroused and inspired by music, music, music,
And this wild-haired music-man became a touch-stone —

Riverflow. . .River-flowing. . .Riversong. . .

The thrill of music swirling in the air,
From my body and through the body of that genius,
Into everyone who had ears to hear his music,

CONTINUE

The people out there in the audience,
Mesmerized, open-mouthed, awakened,
Rising to their feet, applauding,
Carnegie Hall, Philharmonic Hall,
Ahhhh, the thrill of being at once a source,
A receiver, a witness, and a player
Gave life to me then — the freedom of it—
And it lasts to now-here-forever —

Not one memory among others,
But a bedrock source of life-renewal—
A wellspring of ever-running waters, of elixir,
A streaming source from yesterday that becomes
An awakening into my here-now heartsong —
Deep into my forever-moment —
A yesterday with no time,
A now that has no tomorrow —
          Here-now and always yes!

The Riversong from beginning to end,
Flowing smooth and sweet
Like gentle ocean winds whispering
Across quietly singing seas. . .

Because of a plastic radio,
Held to an ear that knew no time,
That early Chet Atkins music and all the music
That has flowed forth during these many years
Is here-now in that forever-moment
Within the river-flow of my streaming life-song. . .

TOGETHER: ONE

I stand on a cliff overlooking the ocean;
Full moon illuminating midnight clouds;
Wind in my face, ocean waves so sweet
So beckoning, so luxuriant in their music.

I have tried to fit, but singers,
Painters and poets travel separately,
Beyond politics, rules, calendars, time.
Our hearts are yours, but we walk alone.

Yet not aloof. To the contrary:
Sing me love and compassion;
Sing me empathy, mercy, hope;
Hold my hand throughout history.

Music sings within us all.
Hope, beauty, joy and love are
Available always. I am with you.

Together: One

RIVER TIME FLOWS TOWARD THE FALLS

Glancing up from my sorrows, seeing
     Seven geese flying serenely above,
     Sliding smoothly in a V, honking —
Vast blue sky, fertile earth below,
     Wings graceful as flowing waters,
     Their wild song a balm for my troubled soul.

As I walked back toward home,
     A hawk drifted on wind-currents,
     Spiraling upward toward the sun,
Swerving lazily into a curve in shining air —
     Daedalus, Whitman, and Jeffers floated
     Into mind, my heart leaped, I smiled.

One moment, life is kisses and rosy cheeks.
     When River Time flows 'round the bend toward the falls,
Sorrows visit empty rooms, solitary meals;
     Dusty shoes; worn shirts; dirty sheets; old soap
     in the dish —
The mind's Bowery offers a wayside bench to lay one's head.
     No door-knocks or telephone calls. Quietude, the
     saving grace.

Honking geese fly serenely in tandem.
     The hawk soars in full flight, a wind-current angel.

     The beauty of our own skysong moment
     Remains forever the giving of compassion —

     The inner light of our silent, observant,
     All-encompassing Witnessing Presence.

SING

Sing my heart for yes, nothing to lose;
Sing for yes, our love-song matters;
You remain the hope,
And yes, there is no other song

And so we sing, finding our way
To courage and its strength —

To the quiet place inside
Where love and light are born.

FOREVER-SONGS

Glances, rings, whispered words,
Songs on the radio, tentative touches,
First kisses, first tongues, first yes —

Forever-songs singing herenow, no loss.

Bless those melodies and the souls
Who cherish, hold and retain them.
Bless those who let them go with a kiss,
A sigh and no regrets. Especially bless
Those who treasure this moment's clarity.

Memorials are made

    By those who sing

Forever-songs

    In our crystalline Now.

FLIGHT OF GEESE

Ah, I can hear them calling.
A flock of geese in flight, beyond the trees.
I rush to the door, open it, walk outside,
Lift my head toward their wild honking.

They appear just beyond the trees,
A magnificent widespread V, each individual attuned to all.
Their voices arise as a melody, each one singing to
The others as they fly like an air-born orchestra.

I crane my head back and listen and watch,
Magnificently attuned with their wild and lofty flight.
My aching heart sings in such deep love
Of their gorgeous beauty, so wild and free.

They honk as they fly across the skies,
Moving slowly into the fog ahead,
Singing their song to me as I watch and listen
As they disappear into grey clouds, distant. . .gone. . .

MOVING THROUGH THE SCRAPBOOKS

Moving through the scrapbooks,
Seeing the memories of myself and others.
Feeling the impact of each image on my soul
Laying me wasted in my past —

As I look, I see a glorious procession of memories —
Football runs, first kisses, playing guitar, Carnegie Hall,
Writing, playing piano, feeling the power of creativity,
The glory, yes, such bliss, yes, such memories, yes.

All of those blissful memories fall into the dark stream
Of past, separate from present: the Now is all, and its bliss is
Magnificent: it contains the sweet songs, the realized hopes,
The disappointed dreams, disillusions, the misguided ef-
forts.

Remembrance is such a sweet delusion.
Memory, so sweet,
Remains a haven for the deluded souls
Who have never found themselves.

Who are we?. . .

NEW MOONS

Dark skies
Shining planets,
Comets in full sail

Where are we —
Memories locked
Dreams continuing
So long ago
> *The we's we were,*
> *The we's we remain.*

Looking at the now
The forever misery,
The forever pains,
The confusions,
The wrenching choices,
Damn, so long to grow —
> *Where are the flowers*
> *We have always been?*

Being in the now — impossible
When beards and breasts are
Growing, budding, becoming
How lovely, sweet the beauty,
How dark the barriers to
Understanding yes, no, choice,
It's all breasts, hair, smiles,
Gorgeous eyes, the promise of
Hope, diving into the green seas.

Such shining light in these new moons.
Such magnificence in these dark skies.
Incredible mystery in these glistening planets —
> *And oh, my god, those sailing comets. . . .*
> *My life in flight, such fire, such beauty. . . .*

WAITING. . .WATCHING. . .LISTENING

Up from the circulating waves emerges
The hem of a dream that came flashing —

      Then disappeared, back into
      The mindstuff of me-mine-more —

      Friend. . . trust. . . hope. . .

      A fluttering of wind and wings
      Creates clouds that swirl through change —
      A saying of goodbyes. . .

Waiting. . .Watching. . .Listening. . .

      As I watch the mind-stream peregrinations,
      Associative dreams released into more dreams,

      And watch a lost and searching me I don't recognize
      Tumbling and turning within my own dream-winds

Waiting. . .Watching. . .Listening. . .

I open my eyes slowly, wondering if ever I can reach
      The point where dreams, drama, and hopes
      Remember the shining power of unity —

A point of committed action
      That gives a bright light
      To any and all who look
Into themselves, and know the natural

      Power of unified wholeness

CONTINUE

Grounded in a heartsong that sings
Of light, love, tenderness, and a strength
That unifies self with others of all musics

With their urgent longings and endless desires...

Waiting...Watching...Listening...

SINGING FOR THE NOW

Wish I could sing a song of love
Wish I could sing a song of light
Wish I could touch the hearts
Of all who live here in my time
And live in all times to come. . . .

Vanity, vanity, vanity, my friend —
Just sing your song of love,
Your song of clear mountain light,
Your song of gentle laughter, yes,
And let the times do whatever they like.

Those who have ears to hear will hear;
The deaf and dumb will not.
Those who have eyes to see will read;
The blind will forever remain alone.
Just love, sing, share, smile, and wave farewell.

DIAMONDFIRE HEARTSONG

Let music with its singing melodies and swirling colors,

Lead us inward, to that still-point center of Clear-Light being.

O, my diamondfire heartsong, sail on music's wings —

From silence all things emerging,

Spinning, spiraling, twirling,

Vanishing, re-emerging,

Receding, transforming —

Cherry blossoms forever dancing,

Humming Kosmos smiling,

Radiant awareness, alive and singing.

LADY OF THE STREAMS

LADY OF THE STREAMS

For Sonia Crespi

The first time here,
She found herself
More lost than found;
She'd known
Brooklyn streets
And drugstore laughter,
Clubroom thrills
And Coney Island wilds,
But what on Earth
Had those to do
With forest streams
And roads of dirt?
New York and L.A.'s
What she'd seen,
Urban provincial,
Subway schooled,
A stranger here
Among these windy pines,
The bluejay kings,
The purple silence
Of the mountains.

With me out there
Fishing pools, and gone,
She felt alone,
Then lonely,
Lost, she thought,
For sure.

CONTINUE

It took awhile, and
Then she found
The Self
She knew
Was there within,
Or so she trusted.
All dropped away
Like veils of Dream--
Glass and steel,
Construction sites,
Neon glitter,
Factory smudge
And roaring bikes--
And there among
The trees and hills
And wind and sky,
She sat upon a rock,
A throne,
Eyes closed,
And breathed
A Universe
Into her soul:
She returned,
Lady Of The Streams.

Shy at first,
Hesitant,
She took a walk

CONTINUE

Alone;
Slowly,
Only slowly,
Did the wind
Entice her heart,
Did trees become
Her friendly sisters,
Stones become
Her guide,
Streams become
Her music,
Earth her feet,
The sky her hair,
A part of her
Already there,
Awakened now,
Alive within/without,
As One:
Sound of water,
Sound of wind,
Sound of Om
Eternal.

She and I
Held hands
Across a stream
Of pretty pools
But dangerous rocks,

CONTINUE

Slippery, cold and wet,
Not large,
Steppingstones
By chance.
She took the leaps,
Including those
She didn't think
She could,
And climbed
The slopes beyond,
Eyes brightly smiling,
Backpack tight,
Her new boots
Hiking trails
And over logs and stones:
She called the flowers friends.

A fire or two
We'd made together;
This time, though,
She built the fire
Herself.
Near the stream
Where I was fishing,
She circled stones
And gathered wood;
Smoke curled up
From oak and aspen twigs,

CONTINUE

From pine she fired herself.
The trout she cooked
Were wild and sweet
In open air,
Just like the love
We made beneath
The pines and
Deep blue sky. . .

Her tree's Blue Spruce,
My Lady Of The Streams,
And now she calls
The mountains home,
And smiles each time
She dreams.

THE WAYS OF TIME AND JOY

For Sonia

Even as we joy these days
  They fly beyond our grasp
    But grasping is not our way
      Time spirals on like wind
Cool unstoppable blue

These are the days our hearts sing
    We know the ways of time and joy
The ways our music soars up
      Into air like looping swallows
  Arching into light
    Soon gone, even on the wing,
    Just so

Neither asking nor grasping,
  We savor words, prolong each touch,
    Taste each slice of orange and pear,
      Each sip of tea and crunch of cashew,
Bask in the light of who we are together
  Demanding nothing from existence
    That existence cannot give,
Thrilling in each quiet moment's grace,
  Astonished before the power
    Of our love,
  Where once sickening fear and dark need
Held sway in aching hearts that knew
  Naught but time and death,
  Did not suspect the robust
  Eternity we now know
  Inside this second's passing—

CONTINUE

How grand the new Spring leaves, ever fresh,
How filled with song the canyon winds,
How bright our aging eyes,
Even as we witness orange suns
Descending into shadowed maws

Sitting beside Winter's smartly crackling fire
Watching feathered snowflakes blanket
Dark green pines and leafless oaks,
How warm our hands touching softly,
How easy our smiles and gentle sighs,
How amazing this journey
The wonder of our lives

TOGETHER ALWAYS
For Sonia

That sweet yearning to be with you

    I know so well,

        And yet it's new each time

It's new like Spring's joysmile,

    A cyclic revelation, a startling surprise,

        Well, hello there, who are you?

How beautiful you are with all these years,

    A womanchild, delightful, vibrant,

        Unbroken, still brave, loving, strong

I feel just as shy as you do

    Even with our journeys, memories, and

        Streaming time-winds outside our door

Yes, when we close our eyes and sweep each other

    Into silk and clouds and rushing waters

        We still get lost in bliss, just like we used to

CONTINUE

Who are you? I'll never completely know,

But you're the one I've always loved,

Even before you charmed me

Just by being gentle, the way you see and understand,

The way your strength helps without hurting,

The way you embody compassion, beauty, trust

And so we travel on in love, warmth, joy,

Bright-eyed, smiling, heart-to-heart,

Two as one, together always

LIGHT BEYOND THE SUN

Each day as you feel the fear —
A wrinkle here, a sagging there,
A blind spot here, small aching there —

I stand amazed by your beauty,
Puzzled smile, and trembling lip.

Such a mystery,
Our transient flesh,
Our spirit-sight unwavering.

No song touches my heart more
Than seeing you greet your doubts
With ever-greater love, compassion,
Strength and inner peace.

You, a model of courage and curiosity,
Facing mystery's storm-blue skies,
Clouds roiling black and grey
Across time's shimmer-shifting horizon,

Seeing always the question
Behind the darkness —

Seeing always the question
In the light beyond the sun—

That shines on distant shores
'Cross far-flung other worlds.

NO OTHER LOVE

Awake, alive, aging, yes
Your face, eyes, and hands tell the tale.
Yet your beauty thrills me,

Young as dawn, vibrant as a summer meadow,
Shy, sensuous, lovely —
Coquettish glance, mischievous laugh,
Young within your timesong —

No other love have I
No other smile have I
No other Yes within this life have I

You are the one,
Forever lighting my step,
Yesterday, now, tomorrow —

When I fail to rise
In dawn's early morning,
You will still be here,
In darkness, light, and
Twilight whispers.

These melodious heartsongs
Sing for you, my love,
For you and always you alone. . . .

ONLY YOU KNEW

I could not have asked for more.

Your youth, your smiles,

Your supple breasts and silvery tongue,

Your quiet love when

My squalling doubts

Burst into flames.

You spent yearning nights alone

When my heartfires flowed away —

Torrential words, waterfall music—

Only you knew I could not help it.

You were there, waiting, hoping, trusting

I might emerge from drowning;

You kept alive the strength

That called me like a Siren

Back to you and love.

CONTINUE

∼30∼

And so I spend this hour

Watching suns slide into night,

While you wait in faith, trusting my return.

Sometimes passion is worth the giving

You and I share, an offering, a testament

> *To enduring light.*

Body/Mind

Heartsong

Soul/Light

You gave me everything

And I love you

WE ARE ONE

Passions, yes, verging on departure:
So long, friend, lover, companion, mirror.
So long heartsong, touchsong, visionsong,
Dreamsong, lovesong, the melodies of our lives.

How you turned our life into light.
The magnificence of our bed. Together in the questions
Of our lives. In the sorrows and doubts of our crossroads.
Even in our lost-soul furies we were united in our love.

And now in these moments of departure,
Your music still sings the songs we sang together.
And, yes, we still hold hands and touch lips
Even as timewinds sweep us up and gone.

We are all of everything we have ever known.
We are all of every touch of our eyes in the herenow.
We are all of our youth, our dance, our impassioned intensity,
We are all of every moment we have ever lived and dreamed.

Sing me your song, dear love. I'll sing mine, too.
Even as we grow weaker by the day, our love remains strong.
Here we are, arms open wide, smiles alive and singing —
You-me, yes, together: no other life: we are one.

DRINK, SMOKE, SLEEP

I really don't know
> *Departure's sound or shape.*
When it happens, or how, or what —
> *It's always different, always a surprise.*

Tears well up as I
> *Approach a stop light,*
Hospital behind, future ahead.
> *Rain pattering on the windshield.*

Bed sheets to be changed.
> *Clothes out of the closet.*
Pussycat fed with a new point of view.
> *Favorite songs, remembered touches.*
Silence in the bedroom, rain on the roof.
> *Time distorted. When?...Then?... Now?...*

Lonesome train whistling in the night.
> *No way to transcend time into now.*
No way to transcend now into time.
> *'S all over, baby blue: All about scrapbooks,*
Unwanted dreams, meaningless choices,
> *Night-time on-line escapes, drink, smoke, sleep.*

INTO BOUNDLESS SILENCE

My lady love lay in our bed,

Coughing, gasping, slowly dying,

Her life growing ever smaller

As I stood by helplessly watching.

Each day, as she grew weaker,

I walked down the neighborhood

Sidewalk for my daily exercise,

Knowing her life was ebbing away.

And each day, as I always did,

I stopped to look at the giant

Sunset maple tree that

Grew beside the walkway.

Over the seasons I had watched

The leaves of this great tree

Grow from winter's bare branches

Into sparkling white spring buds

Into great summer green leaves

CONTINUE

That turned to yellow-orange,

Into a gorgeous scarlet celebration.

And when deep autumn arrived,

Its scarlet leaves slowly faded away,

Even as my lady love was fading. . .

Looking up at me from our bed

Her sad eyes brimming with tears

She whispered —

"I love you with all my heart,

But I want to go home now —

I want to go home. . ."

She died the day after Christmas —

I took my walk into the chill air,

My thoughts chaotically jumbled,

My stomach gnarled and churning,

Knowing there was no answer

For any question I could ever ask.

CONTINUE

Stopping by the great red tree

I watched as its very last leaf

Trembled for a brief moment,

Then shuddered, then let go,

Fluttering down to muddy earth.

Since then, I've not been able

   To look at that tree —

No leaves, no joy, no celebration,

   Just naked branches.

Yes, I know Spring will come,

   Bringing new white buds

   And golden-scarlet leaves. . .

But, oh, my lady love,

   The love of my life,

Is borne on winter's dark wind

   Into that boundless silence

That lasts on. . . and on. . .

     Forever. . .

THIS TEAR-DROP MOMENT

I look upon the beauty of the young ones
Of my remembered youth, rebellion, curiosity.
She who recognized and touched me;
Awakening me to love, a new reality.

Sing me those sweet songs of who and what we were;
Those music-moments of our long-ago time. . . .
She who sang to me and wooed my heart, whose
Music awakened my body-mind-soul to light and love.

She who felt my own music, too, and moved with me
In the songs and melodies and fierce arenas in which
We sang and danced across the stages in our glorious youth —
Sing me again, oh sweet memories, do not forget...

Not then, but now, feeling her here with me,
Not yesterday but in this living moment, still alive —
Yes, sing me your siren song once more, as I dive deeply
Into this tear-drop moment, feeling you with me always.

FOREVER

Out into the clouded nightsky
Far away from TV's madness,
Into the quietude of dark skies
Silent houses, the spacious night.

Remembered songs we sang still ring —
The times we lived and hearts we loved,
The magic in our words and music
Ring true to me every time I hear them.

Bless us all, the passions we felt, so young,
The freedoms we touched, lived, celebrated —
Not lost on me. . . Forever in my heartsong . . .
Oh, holy night, oh, holy moments, oh, holy love.

The magic and beauty and celebratory reality
Of those singing, love-making moonlit nights
Lived then, lived now, living forever in the heart
Of treasured memories . . . A moment, a touch, a melody —

Time has no curse on reality: we live forever.
How her smile beguiled me, how her kiss awakened me;
How the moonlight caressed my body near the river
As she touched me and kissed my innocent mind —

The music

And the moonlight

Thrilled me

Forever. . . . Forever. . . . Forever. . . .

LOVE AND GRIEF

You love your cat
      rise
      rise
      rise
She dies
      down
      down
      down
You love your wife
      rise
      rise
      rise,
She dies: darkness
      Spreads,
      Spreads,
      Spreads
Crumbling source —
      Heart, center, soul—
      Reduced to tears
      To trembling ash
Ashes die
      Die into blue
      Blue shade
Blue shade dim
      Dimmer still
      Into purple light
      Falls the night
Love and grief
      Tied
      Tied
      Tied
  Together

GOODNIGHT KISSES

After all the love, all the care,
All the commitments and promises
Came the darkness, an empty midnight.

After all the questions and answers
All the assertions and arguments,
After all the distinctions, logic, proofs —

Look out to ocean swells shimmering in moonlight,
Into the silence beyond unmet needs,
Beyond doubts, anxieties, wishes, desires —

There lies relief. . .release. . .peace. . .

Would I could rest forever in the bliss
Of my lover's arms after goodnight kisses

NEW YELLOW FLOWERS

New yellow flowers rise in Springtime grass
White buds wave on the red maple's branches
My heart still aches — memory cannot dim it
I walk with divided mind, trying to listen
To the birds sing joy even as my tears yearn to flow.

Passing by a bush I see moisture gleaming
On a leaf — I stop, look at a single large bead,
Bend nearer to it, nearer still, watching the world
Within it expand as I fall into it, begin to disappear,
Losing any sense of out here, becoming engulfed.

I stand there, shivering in the Spring wind,
Lost in another world, the world within that drop,
Mindless, thoughtless, separate from self,
Freed from memories of love, misery, pain, loss.
Pulling away, I look around, dizzy, feeling faint.

Then I heard a bird singing joyously as it flew
Directly across my vision. I looked around and saw
New yellow flowers rising and singing in Springtime grass.
I looked at the red maple tree and its new white buds
Dancing in the wind, felt my tears draw back, and smiled. . .

LEAVE A CANDLE BURNING

Turn out the lights, but leave a candle burning,
Knowing that those who have left us remain with us.
With our eyes closed, let us open our hearts, and
Let the memories flood into us, crystal clear,
As if we and they were still with us, here, now, forever.

Even knowing there is no forever, let us feel their presence;
Let us know that in their passing our passing is with them.
Know that our living remains an acceptance of the dying;
And the dying affirms our living in our living moment.
Even as we look backward, before our time, so too we look
Directly into the maw that has preoccupied us since the beginning.

So turn out the lights. Leave a single candle burning.
Let that light illuminate our mind's shadows, and let us
Celebrate the life that gives us our life, and celebrate as well
The death of ourselves we have for so long denied.

Life is the illumination of that silent world from which we came.
That silent world has given birth to you, to me, and to all
Of the flowers, birds' wings, songs of children, and our joyful dance.
Sing not of loss, my friend, but of celebration,
            and may that candle burn on.

LISTEN WITHOUT THOUGHT

Come walk with me
   Just for a while
Let's leave the city's angry traffic,
   Desperate competition, perpetual noise —
Leave behind our memories, desires,
   And all those ancient fears
      Just for a while

Let us walk this dirt road
   To the pond's quiet waters,
Looking at autumn's leaves,
   Seeing their reds and golds;
Listening to the breeze,
   Hearing its music and feeling its
Cool caress on our cheeks

Let us stand beside still waters
   And release the ways
   Of mind and time,
   Finding within our quietude
The sights, songs and sounds
   Of life with water, sky, and
   Autumn's gentle passing —

Be here for the moment,
   Moving into sound;
Look for a while,
   Learn how to see;
No mind, no time —
   Listen without thought

CONTINUE

And hear the inner bell chiming
  Unmoored,
  We now stand free
From the self that once was here,
  The remembered self,
  A dream dreaming itself,
Images of lives lived somewhere else
  By someone else with people who once
  Were here, now there, now gone. . . .
    The floating life,
    Songs written on water
    Cast into mind-sky,
    Rising into dimming light,
Vanishing in morning's mist. . . .

RIVERRUSH TO STILLPOINT

Spring's silver riverrush thrillspills my yearning soul,

Tumble-spins consciousness, shaking brainfueled skull,

Liberates hesitating linguist, heaves my red and yellow birds,

Gives breathlife, vital courage, siphoned energy,

Wings to words, singwing-soaring, whippy-diving, swoosh-arising

Skysailing up-through-beyond cliffcloudsclimbing, into infinite blue

Ocean alive, love-rush crying, celebrate attunement shining Now,

Yea, yip, yawping foxes leaping 'cross the green in frolictime,

Energyjoysong rivulet, rushing south in creeks, bursting streams,

The riverrush again, thrillspilling heart-soul rising

Brightlight greeting heron-cries across the sundown marshes,

Riverrush my breathless leaping wherebegone, howbegone, whybegone

Songtothemoon

Ocean sailorwinds full sails blowblast,

Mountain aspen treewind bending across and down the slopes

Harkly howly-yowling nature's joydance,

Jumply-upward, clicking heels in rushwind skyblue clearlight air,

CONTINUE

Suddenly suspended, alive and radiant,

Wind stops —

Eternal moment, herenow fixed,

Glorious still-point

Silent in the sun

HEAT, HEART, AND FIRE

HEAT, HEART, AND FIRE

How sweet the body's touch,
Release, escape, transcendence;
But more, the mindscape —
Imagination's fulfillment —
Desires, passions, electro-whispers,
Swirling images, vivid dreams alive

I have known all before, and now I know
Language transcending language —
Boundaries obliterated, body aflame,
Freedom expressed, sonic vibrance,
Touch made heat, heart, and fire.

Distance on map-space,
Nearness through on-line keyboards,
Zero distance through heartsong intimacy,
Real-time electro-singing mind-touch,
Transcendent word-flight, sex-song beauty.

ELECTRIC WORDS

You so young; me, white-hair now;
You, so Yes Oh Yes; me, wondering How;
You so vibrantly bringing us alive;
The two of us, lost and found in electric words.

Words singing through air and wires,
Touching mind directly, piercing walls,
Moving without light, flesh, rules —
Impassioned, arousing, fierce, singing. . . .

Singing songs, singing body-mind touch;
Words touching breasts, ears, tongues,
Touching knees, thighs, hair, mind,
Zones alert, pulsing, throbbing, alive.

Electric words, space vibrations,
Music-whispers, faceless, sightless,
Words enlivening breasts, thighs, tongues,
Space-words igniting heat-songs, flesh-fire.

Sing to me, lover, yes. I am with you. Your songs
Touch my mind, my body, my heart,
Make my blood sing with a life of its own —
Bless you, darlin', here, yes, a thousand miles away.

NITE RYDER DREAM-SONGS

Is there no way out
Of self, mind, reason,
Convention, words, order,
Lists, maps, numbers?

Give me fierce intensity, electricity,
Visual illumination — more.

Seeking deliverance,
Mind-flight freedom,
Dreamtime relief,
        Electric brain,
            Poetry on fire.

Give me ecstatic bliss,
Psycho-sonic intensity,
Liberation from legality, conformity,
Lukewarm mundane life-as-it-is.

Incinerate moderation!
Give me inflamed imagination,
Sexual intensity, release, relief,
Escape from convention, barriers, and
This moment's meaningless wasteland.
            Rise up!

Celebrate those mad
Intoxicated lovers who give their lives
To passion, touch, sexuality, beauty,
Heat, and brainfire transcendence. . . .

Through darkland shades,
Shadows, questions, doubts,
My Nite Ryder dream-songs
Wing me into blinding light.

SUNLIGHT'S INVALUABLE PROMISE

In the loneliness of the death night
Where do we go? Memory remains
A living tomb, a cauldron of dreams,
Passions, heartsongs, bliss and tears.

Do we say Hello to new faces?
Do we reach out beyond our covid masks?
Do we pretend to care when all seems lost?
Bless the love goddess appearing in darkest night.

Speak to me, my friend, speak to me my heart;
You who know and feel and respond to my needs.
Yes, speak to me, shedding human masks that have
Imprisoned humanity from childhood to the coffin.

There are ways. We have walked forests wild,
Crossed familiar paths, embraced rules, regulations.
There comes a time when social shackles must be shed,
When passions deep and true must finally be celebrated.

Sing me a song of passion, love goddess. Release emotions,
Streams, fountains, fervent songs and psycho-sexual energies
That inflame the mind, awaken sex-fires, those holy connections
That vitalize humanity, and you, and me, in our shared loneliness.

You're a voice, a vision, a presence whom I have never seen or touched,
You are with me in midnight moments of loneliness, isolation, desperation,
Personal misery, blessing me, saving me, giving me strength:
Allowing my deepest, truest, most impassioned moments their songs.

CONTINUE

*Yes, there are those goddesses who live lonely lives
And yet share their loving compassion with us lost ones,
Who keep personal kisses to themselves, yet give to those
In need her rare mind and hope-filled, energizing presence.*

*Bless the givers, the lovers who nourish, uplift, and save the lives
Of those on the fringe, the brink, the dizzying edge of insanity;
Those of us lost, verging on madness in a darkening wilderness.
She's a goddess dancing; her song is sunlight's invaluable promise.*

WORD-TOUCH ELECTRONIC FIRE

Lonely room
Empty bed, covers cold,
Your room dark and lonely,
His room alight, no love.

Open your iphone,
An electronic world awakens,
Opens eyes, ears, senses,
Digital space aflame, timeless

Lovers singing, connecting
Minds, hearts, feelings,
Abstract body-mind,
Flesh awakened, word-touch

Word-touch alive, quivering
Mind-talk, sensual, true,
Mind-talk, you-me-us,
Brain-fire alive, vibrant, visual,

Beyond self, connected, floating
Word-touch, body-music, mind-heart
Flesh-songs merging, senses streaming,
Singing hearts linked, melding,

Sex-love singing in the mind-song —
Word-touch, relief, breath, relief,
Whispers, relief, singing-sex, yes,
Herenow, yes, electronic fire.

BEAUTIFULLY AND TRULY FOREVER

I sing our dreams,
The beauty we envisioned,
Our touch, tongues and glances —
The way we whisper-sang our heart-songs.

But take a moment,
Let's not fall in love quite yet —
I sing Yes our song, but I sing and cry
Our universal human heart-song as well.

When I think of you,
Deep kisses, warm, wet, wild,
Lying beside you, skin to skin,
Hand to face, to breast, to thigh,
Yes, when I think of you,
I think of our vivid passion-dreams,
Our touch, whispers, feel-me emotions —

But how can you possibly love me?
My guitar, my songs and my poems know no home —
I sing for each and all of us, without name or eyes,
Our desires, our loves, our cares, not one but all.

How sweetly you and I kiss and touch, so softly unite —
Our singing (such beauty in our nightlight)
Enfolded as one in heart and depth;
Moving and swaying our pulsesong's ocean tides.

I am Yes, but not for love.
I am merely a wandering troubadour,
A reclusive poet, a singer of songs ,
Here, there, everywhere, soon gone.

CONTINUE

Our loving music drifts in nightlight;
Our fleeting history swirls like wind;
Our beautiful moments, forever Yes and Yes —
Absorbed in the rush of a thousand tomorrows.

You remain deep within me,
And sing these sweet melodies attuned with me.
We have merged our hearts — Let us embrace
Our moments, beautifully and truly forever.

SWEET ANGELS

Reminded of Anthony Quinn looking up
At the infinite overwhelming night-sky —
La Strada, last scene, absolutely alone
Overwhelmed by isolation in the vastness.

Midnight. . . age. . .loss of lover, best friend. . .
Music swelling . . . piano. . . into my night,
Music sounding, music felt, music lost in the now.
Music singing what is alive in that same moment.

All a rush of compressed time —
Childhood, youth, teens, college,
Efforts toward direction, purpose. . .
Takes awhile for deep music to surface.

Oh, yes, those glorious songs of our time —
The expression, the acceptance, the Yes,
The adulation, the applause,
The fulfillment of the grandest heartsongs . . .

Now, at this time, memories not enough —
Bright, beautiful, stimulating, but
In the end, distant empty echoes,
Reflections of an exhausted mind.

Thank god for goddesses who appear
By chance for us lost broken warriors,
For us cast-off lonely lovers. Thank god
For our vital angels who understand. . .

CONTINUE

Kiss, comfort, welcome —
Who understand touch in the lonely night
Who understand how the heart aches —
Hold me, wordless, hear my heartbeat. . . .

We who find ourselves aged, wrinkled,
Finally afraid of it all, find ourselves
Profoundly grateful for those angelic ones who
Seek, find and love us in the shadows and bless us.

A revitalization of it all; beyond memory,
Into present moment's electric fire;
New life, beyond past, into now, proud, erect,
Grateful: thank you, sweet angels who know.

SEEK ME AND FIND YOURSELF

When love comes my way,
My gratitude knows no bounds.
If love becomes need, I shy away,
For need grasps, binds, constricts.

Let us move beyond, embracing all.

Daily life seems far from
These heights. Looking out
Over lakes, distant mountains,
Red-orange clouds and sunsets,

I breathe clear, clean air,
Distant but not heartless;
Separate but near; aware, yet
Warm, empathic, loving, kind.

From within, I witness our desires,
Our sufferings, hopes and dreams.
My heart opens wide, embracing all
Within our shared tears and laughter.

When another reaches out to touch me,
Raises a finger to stroke my cheek,
I move back slightly, not abiding the
Personal moment, the possessing gesture.

CONTINUE

Do not look into my eyes and tell me your name.
Look into my eyes and soar beyond your name.
Ask not sympathy for your immediate trials.
Sing me your deepest life-song, and I sing with you.

Fear and misery hypnotize, but pass away. Passions
Transform tears into hopes and new dreams.
I, the Witness, stand within your deepest shrine,
Aware, alert, observant. Seek me and find yourself.

A RINGING MOUNTAIN GONG

It's easy to sit back, smile,

And raise a glass, a toast,

"Let's keep on keepin' on"—

But behind the smile and the toast

A tragedy slowly erodes the soul —

The hero strides forth in power,
Bravely confronts his dragons,
Wins his battles, then sits back,
And welcomes the cheers,

The applause and kisses

Of his devoted followers.

But age and time are taking their toll —
The loss of talent and courage,

The loss of friends and true love,
The loss of body, mind and soul —

Yes, they are taking
Their toll, even on him.

He stands next in line

To drop to his knees,

CONTINUE

Pitching forward,

Hands outstretched,

Clutching nothing but

Sand, dust, and ashes.

He too dies the death

Of all who walk the Earth

   In pride, misery, shame

    Ignorance or awareness.

But for now,

(Even when his heart is lost

And weeping its forever-song)

He can smile, laugh,

Raise his glass, and

Speek as loudly and

Clearly as a ringing mountain gong —

"Let's just keep on keepin' on!

I WILL NEVER FADE AWAY

I will never fade away —
 My guitar sang my love for you
 My piano soared to the heavens
 Every word I've ever written
 Has been for you and you alone
I'll never fade away

I will never fade away —
 My time is near
 I'll soon be done and gone
 But my words shall ring
 My music will sing on for you
I will never fade away

I'll remember our song 'til I die
When I die, I will be gone,
But my love for you is so strong
That it will never fade away

When you recall in the now
 A line I wrote that moved you,
 That strikes a note in your heart,
 Even as you hear it now, you will awaken,
As if suddenly — and you will know

CONTINUE

I will never fade away
   My time is near
I will be done and gone
   But my words shall ring
In your heart like
   A distant mountain bell

And my music will sing on for you

   I will never fade away

WALKING, WITH NEW EYES

Walking the same sidewalk
Past the same houses
The same trees
The same bushes,
Seeing each tree,
Bush, leaf and house

Shining inside a soft glow —

When we look through new eyes.

One day in autumn's wind

The leaves have fallen,
The earth is dark, barren,
The dying flowers bend,
The dark sky rumbles,

The air offers no life or love.

The next day, it's spring

And the sap rises
From deep in the earth,
Up the trunk of the tree,

Bursting into new white flowers
That sing aloud the joyful
Song of life, love and beauty.

Walking quietly, paying attention,
Watching every moment of every

CONTINUE

Transmission from root, to flower,
To the living song of life itself,
Makes all the difference in the
Way we feel, the way we become,
The way we live our lives

From moment to moment,

Day to day, year to year—

In silent awareness, we walk

Looking with those fresh new eyes,

Seeing all that is familiar with

An alertness that embraces

All we see and think and do

From moment to moment,

To each second of each moment

To the end of life and time itself.

THE CLOSING CHAPTER

The rains came, and he walked

Shirtless, hatless, no shoes,

Weeping in the misery of his loss —

Struggling to grow above and beyond

The endless images in his mind —

Her smile, her loving beauty,

Her gentle touch, her laughter.

All this pain, all this struggle —

Walking in the rain, weeping,

Cursing the night and his life.

Time, time, more time passed,

In which he sat home alone,

Reading books without thinking;

Watching television mindlessly;

Drinking and smoking too much —

And then the moment arrived when

He awoke as if from a bad dream.

He suddenly saw his way — a narrow

Pathway through the rain,

Through that god-awful night.

CONTINUE

He began a journey, sure-footed,

Along the narrow path that led away

From the past, toward the future.

He thought not of what lies below,

Of losing his grip and falling

Into those sorrowful memories,

But of here and now and of

What maybe, just perhaps, lies ahead.

A bright light suddenly blinded him:

Everything lies ahead, he realized:

There is no past, only an ascending now

That moves endlessly upward.

He stopped thinking about

What he had failed to do,

And about what he could do.

At that moment, he felt peace.

He felt serenity. Imagination

Is everything, he thought, as he

 Sat down and began writing once again.

RIVERSONGS

WATCHING

Like any artist, I watch myself.
Revealing much, not all.

True singing is from the heart.

Not only watching, but watching
Myself watching myself watching.

Lead me deeper, shadow friend.

On daily walks, observing
The color of air; new flowers waving.

Sing to me. Whisper-touch my bodymind, too.

I react and react to my reacting,
Observing myself observing myself reacting.

Take me deeper, into my song's heartbeat.

The all-seeing eye; slow breezes rustling leaves —
Spring leaves, summer leaves, autumn leaves.

Close my eyes, dream me, drift me deeper.

Leaves poised, fading, falling, gone.
In my knowing, my time comes too.

Sing me, touch me, help me release the song of Now,
Embracing yes, no, here, now, this moment. . . gone.

A FLAME-SPEAR'S LIGHT

Crickets outside, singing, autumn night,
Big trees swaying, leaves turning red
Cold morning air, heat on,
Smoke like fog, orange California fires.

Silence in distant night,
Silence in the air, in the mind,
Silence within our chaotic times —
Hear madness throbbing
Within television's sound-waves —

But in the music of my soul: quietude.

All around, in the world's sphere,
Swirling misery, whirling chaos.
Within the center, a flame-spear's light —
Eye-song: watcher: singing here the sight.

Hands above keyboard, waiting,
Melodies dancing, weaving, singing —
There are no moments other than music.
All is music: how we listen, how we hear.

Temple wind-chimes ring within the heartsong.
Dance in light, close your eyes, raise your arms,
Listen, hear, and sway to the singing bells.

RIVERSONG

The river keeps reaching, but never reaches
Each moment is here, is now, is gone
It arrives but for an instant, flows on,
And here we are, remaining, watching,
Waiting, wondering, living, and seeking
The yesterday that is now today,
Lost and found in the sound of the riversong.

I met a woman, lovely, beautiful,
She said yes, we loved,
We became memories, lost
In the music we heard then,
And hear now, a breath of air,
A sigh, a dream that touches
The heart just as fresh as
That first touch that remains
Like the river flowing in the now,
Forever singing my heartsong.

Each song I hear on the radio;
Each song I hear from the TV;
Each song I hear from there, to here,
Rings a chime, a bell, a note that
Awakens a song I've known before
But remains here and now within me,
Ringing memories that live as fresh
As new morning light, as a tear-drop
That sings the song of then but is now.
And even as I hear those sweet songs
Playing now the way they played then,
I sink back into the river's flow,
The time that is here-now forever.

CONTINUE

The riversong is my song,
A song of here and now, of then,
Of tomorrow, of yesterday,
Of a tomorrow that will never
Leave me, even as the radio,
The TV, and all of the means
Of today's world will bring me
Ever closer to the then that is now,
And to the now that is forever then.

WITHIN THIS SHINING NOW

After checking-in to Facebook,
After enjoying the pussycats,
The mountains and oceans,
The sunsets and wisdom-words,

I need to visit my isolation —
This blank page throws me into myself,
Into my yesterdays, todays, tomorrows,
Into my Eternal Now.

Past, future, present, vanish into
Into a still and timeless grace —
Quietude, a mountain stream,
Soft breezes rustling aspen leaves.

And here in this eternal moment,
Separate from sorrows and isolation,
The misery of our epoch vanishes:
Within this shining Now: blissful peace.

ALL THINGS FLOW

Sitting in the studio,
Feeling our times,
Singing the music
Of our shared soul:

Listen up. Shake off the
Personal, miserable ego —
Debts, fears, lusts,
Doubts, projected horrors —

Settle back, release, relax.
Close eyes. Breathe deeply.
Separate self from not-self.

Our great anxiety?

Bliss will pass. This, too,
Shall flee, flit and fly.

Betwixt fear and realization
All things flow into a new now.

One moment. One song,
Infinite variations.

THE THOUSAND-YEARS WOES

The thousand-years woes are upon me now —
How it is that today is yesterday's hope,
Revealing the truth of time's smile,
How they merge into a single moment,
And here I am, lost between memory and tomorrow.

The great ones speak to me of time and the now.
I understand them clearly. When I'm walking my walk,
I lose my self into the majesty of flowers blooming,
Trees coming alive from buds to blossoming flowers —

And then lose my self until my self returns,
And once again, I'm lost in the me I've always been,
A searching soul who at best can touch the center
And find the universal me, just before I vanish into eternity.

Awareness makes the difference between now and tomorrow's then.
Aware, I find myself bridging the mind-gap between yes & no,
Like & dislike, preferring this, opposing that —
I stand above it all, a whole being: a witnessing mirror.

Transcending opposites, I emerge into selfless awareness,
Seeing clearly, without preferences, I become the mirror,
Complete, free of self, radiant and fully alive.

How good it feels to accept the memories, all the mistakes,
Errors, failures, and all of the triumphs, victories and trophies, too.

Putting them into the past, they transform into a new now.
I can accept them into my heart, and let my heart bloom —

CONTINUE

Yes and no become a single yin/yang yes, a complete unity
And all of the love I have given — and received.

I just wish that those thousand-years woes did not descend —

That I could welcome my loss of hair,
The weakening in my legs, my eyes going,
My inevitable descent into the grave:

But that descent has its own beauty.
Yes, every year closer to the grave
Is also ever year closer to the fulfillment
Of every note I have played,
Every word I have written

STAND WITHIN THE STARS

Stand within the stars and behold the beauty —

Open your eyes, spread your arms, breathe,

Disappear into that magnificence,

Breathe again, let your thoughts fly up and away,

Breathe still again and release your mind.

Release your self, your personal burdens.

Let them fly away into that firmament, release,

Yes, release once more, and clear your mind,

Give it all up, the clutter, the worry, the madness,

The clutchings, the holdings, the miseries,

All of the concerns that keep you tethered, tied,

Captured, chained, bound, jailed, alone.

Out beneath those astonishing stars,

Let yourself be astonished. Breathe in, breathe out,

Release, relax, let go, set yourself free: sweet liberation.

CONTINUE

Never have you known such release, such freedom

Such deep relaxation, liberation, breathing free and clear.

Forget your freeway drives, your television news,

Forget your boss, your schedules, the papers on your desk;

For just these moments look up at that magnificent skyscape

And find yourself liberated, free, and whole and perfect

In these ecstatic moments of breathing, seeing, participating

In Universal beauty, truth, freedom, life, love, understanding —

All things beautiful, divine, universal, and profoundly whole.

Rarely have we known such moments. Oh, yes —

Power's exhilaration; triumph's ecstasy; sex's thrill,

Personal domination, competition's victory, the ecstasy

Of power triumphing over power — passing illusions,

Fleeting thrills. . .gone. . . leaving only emptiness.

CONTINUE

Set yourself aside and, yes, for at least a moment,

Stand within the stars and behold their beauty —

Open your eyes, spread your arms, breathe,

Disappear, let thoughts soar up and away,

Breathe once more — let your wingéd spirit fly.

TAO

Within intensity,

The calm.

Within quietude,

The flame.

Motion in repose

Cessation in motion

Serenity in action —

Music Source

THE CANOE RIDER

Just a fellow riding his canoe
Down the river toward the falls,
Noting the banks of either side —

The bank of Yes, the bank of No;
The bank of White, the bank of Black;
The bank of Day, the bank of Night.

No shaggy mountain-top guru;
No high-hatted Catholic priest;
No red-robed Buddhist chanter.

Just a wandering musician-poet;
Enjoying the waters, the sun, the light;
The river he rides uniting both banks as One.

ABOUT THE POET

During the late '60s and early '70s, after graduating from San Francisco State College with a degree in English Literature, Lee Underwood played lead guitar with singer/songwriter Tim Buckley on seven of the nine albums Buckley released while alive, including Happy Sad and Starsailor. Underwood also appeared on several posthumous Buckley CDs, notably Dream Letter: Live in London 1968 and Works In Progress. He toured America and Europe with Buckley for seven years, and in 2002 published a book entitled Blue Melody: Tim Buckley Remembered (Backbeat Books).

While living in Los Angeles with Sonia Crespi in the '70s and '80s, Underwood wrote extensively about music and musicians. His articles, interviews and reviews appeared in dozens of periodicals, including Down Beat (West Coast Editor, 1975-1981), L.A. Times, L.A. Weekly, Rolling Stone, Pulse, Jazz Forum, L.A. Free Press, New Realities, Body/Mind/Spirit, New Age Journal, and many others. In 1990, he co-authored flutist Paul Horn's autobiography, Inside Paul Horn (HarperCollins; 1990), and in 1991 received the Crystal Award for Music Journalism at the NAM Convention in Hollywood.

During the '90s, Lee and Sonia moved to Rio En Medio, a small town outside of Santa Fe, where they lived in a small hand-built adobe house for seven years. During that time, they drove all about New Mexico and southern Colorado, camping by streams and hiking in the mountains. It was a heavenly time for them, and a major influence in Underwood's writing.

From there, they moved to Oakhurst, CA in 1997, where they lived for 20 years in the mountains, in a large house beside a year-round stream. It was here that Lee wrote two books of poetry — Timewinds (PM Books 2010) and Diamondfire (Outskirts Press 2016). In 2017, Underwood and his beloved wife Sonia Crespi moved to Petaluma, CA. Here, Underwood wrote Into Light (Poetic Matrix Press, 2021).

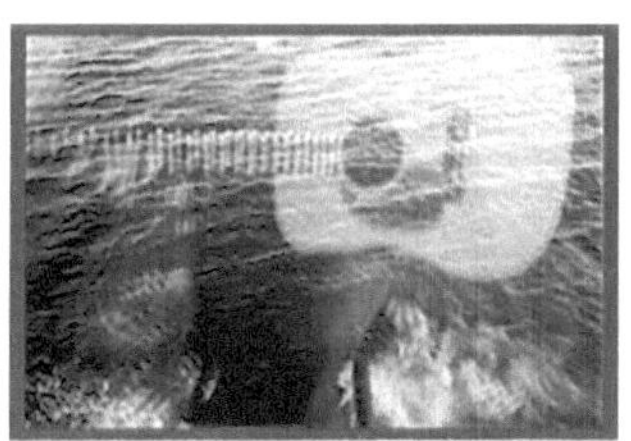